The Magic of the Mind

Rebecca Blume

The Magic of the Mind

Vanguard Press

VANGUARD PAPERBACK

© Copyright 2023
Rebecca Blume

The right of Rebecca Blume to be identified as author of this work has been asserted by them in accordance with the Copyright, Designs and Patents Act 1988.

All Rights Reserved

No reproduction, copy or transmission of this publication may be made without written permission.
No paragraph of this publication may be reproduced, copied or transmitted save with the written permission of the publisher, or in accordance with the provisions of the Copyright Act 1956 (as amended).

Any person who commits any unauthorised act in relation to this publication may be liable to criminal prosecution and civil claims for damages.

A CIP catalogue record for this title is available from the British Library.

ISBN 978 1 83794 027 1

Vanguard Press is an imprint of
Pegasus Elliot Mackenzie Publishers Ltd.
www.pegasuspublishers.com

First Published in 2023

Vanguard Press
Sheraton House Castle Park
Cambridge England

Printed & Bound in Great Britain

REFLECTIONS:

Part I

As my mind untangles, the imprisonment of my mania finds freedom in the structure and stability that surrounds me. It is the power of positivity that has once again launched me forward into a life of hope, faith, and love. By slowly peeling back my darkness and the secrets that consumed me and with a willingness for growth, I now find myself quickly sprinting towards a new kind of freedom. A freedom distant from a sense of imprisonment. A freedom full of excitement and anticipation instead of freshly out of a place of fear, pain, and trauma. I now believe in myself and my ability to live a life of independence, accountability and with a moral compass full of fulfilling values.

As the torture of my mind fades, I sit quietly and listen to the peaceful sound of the air instead of the voices in my head. I find comfort, safety, and security in my breath and in my very being. I find freedom in my soul and an openness to vulnerability that allows for feeling once again. All my needs have been met and it is in my hands only to follow through. My pattern of insanity has already been broken. That is not the problem. My commitment to self, though, is a mere desire. I want a connection. I want love. I want freedom. I cannot attract these desires because I want them. It takes work, and this time, I want to fight.

What we, as humans, are capable of enduring is nothing less than a miracle. Living one life may be enough, but to live many takes work. With grace and dignity, I walk away from the web of lies and deceit that once filled me with shame and guilt. I walk into the light; a place where I have been before. The familiarity brings me back to the innocence and purity of my childhood and the freedom of my laugh sings to my desire for a forever youthful soul.

This time, I am here to stay.

By immersing myself in present time, my ability to overcome grief has transitioned from repetitive, long nights of agonizing shrieks to a quick cry followed by an acceptance and understanding of hardships that once perceived as unfair, now are found with gratitude and growth. Amid my delusions, everything I feel, see, and hear and the synchronicities that unfold are my reality, my truth and in my insanity, believed to be signs that ultimately throw me into a vicious and persistent fight for proof and truth.

With my newfound emotional and self-awareness, my ability to grieve the insanity of my truth is now a battle easily won. Reflecting on the cycle of my past grief that defeated me and my idea of the power of love that consumed me, I see a sad girl desperately looking for fantasy and escape.

To now have a satisfaction that calms my impatience and a hope that is undying, I sit in my discomfort with confidence and belief that what is meant to be will unfold when the time is right. By leaving behind the thought that I deserve something extraordinary and that I am extraordinary, I find comfort and peace in knowing I am a small speck of light in this expansive universe filled with shining stars, shooting stars and more unknowns than my mind can comprehend.

Presently, I desire and dream of miracles. And so does my insanity.

The fields of my mind were once overwhelmed with weeds that I carelessly left to expand and grow between isolated and scattered flowers that I fought to reach while pushing myself through high and wild grasses with an unawareness that left me blind to the crystal-clear streams just beyond the chaos of my frazzled and lost mind. As my oblivion searched for openings where there would be expansive fields of flowers fully in bloom and trickling waters full of life, I was only discovering small patches of buds needing water and sun until I surrendered and stumbled aimlessly upon a space full of freedom where endless flowers were opening and reaching their petals towards the sun.

I was not alone in this field of dreams. I found family, friends and an unconditional love that pranced through my soul and gave me a deeper meaning that inspired me to return to the scary fields and rip out the weeds. I no longer got lost in the trauma of my suffocating insanity and fear of support and asked this love to accompany me back to the ugly and evil fields where I received help unrooting the past and then was guided back to where family and friends patiently waited for my return.

As I became comfortable in this new place, I became comfortable exploring the beauty within it. My eyes opened wide to the colors and movement of nature. I moved safely throughout this sacred field with the intention of covering all the ground and with the hope of touching every flower, only to pick the ones that caught my eye and brought physical feelings to my heart. I saw my reflection in the streams. A beauty never seen before overwhelmed my emotions and I searched fearlessly to feel all that is possible; good, bad and the impossible.

Beauty is powerful.

I dance to the rhythm of my beating heart, find movement from every song and as I open my soul and hear every layer of music, the feelings from all my sensitive senses explode with freedom and joy. I try to find self-expression in everything I do: with gestures, my voice, movement, and any creative outlets I can express. I no longer feel the need to be altered into a more comfortable and relaxing mindset to embrace the humility that now dances through my soul and exudes confidence and a careless freedom that shines for all to see.

I want to attract the best. I want to approach, be approached, and remain approachable while embodying a kind, sincere and genuine character. I want to enlighten and be enlightened while remaining curious with no judgment and with an open mind that soaks up knowledge while sifting quickly through the different perspectives and attaining only what applies to my interests and values. I want to be moved. I wanted to be stimulated. I want to be tested.

My freedom of expression portrays a vision of colorful fashion and unbrushed hair. I take ownership of my free spirit which will continue to dance through life towards love, connection and a freedom that lives deep within us all, and as I shovel the hard and rocky dirt out of the external masks we all wear, I hope to hit the bottom where authentic beauty and vulnerability are alive, a fragile and real place where a scary reality of insanity and dreams resides.

Let's show our faces.

I wake early arising from a small bed that has surrounded me with safety and warmth, and as I bounce out of the comforts of my dreams, I feel alive and ready for another day where I strive to comfort others with the warmth, I have been grateful to receive and maintain. I greet each day with a positivity and light that I believe has kept me alive during sleepless, dark times of nightmares where extreme spikes of chills and heat possessed my cold then hot defeated body.

The now balanced temperature within my soul sheds an energy of equality and stability. I see the gifts we all possess and without shoving them in faces in hopes for them to be passionately ripped open and revealed, I instead place them sensitively under a tree where they sit patiently and remain visible until approached and peeled open when the time has come.

I give my heart deeply and I give my input sparingly. Let us feel our gifts. Let our minds not overwhelm us. Let us own our stories and live in the present where every night we fall into a deep sleep full of beautiful dreams that we wake to reflect upon and then return to the excitement of each unknown moment that today will bring and tomorrow will reveal.

Life is the greatest gift of all.

My carelessness and impulsivity, which once accelerated self-sabotage have now shifted to a carelessness in opposition that screams in anger at my past self-destruction and now whispers calmly to a content soul that all will be okay. That is what it is. That I have no control of my history and that the past is the past. That I had tough cards dealt with in life and that it is not my fault. That the regrets I question should be had, I don't want and so don't exist.

I move from place to place with the intention of finding a place called home. A place of stability. A place that welcomes the chaos of a life full of babies. Full of family. Full of traditions and memories. Full of a love that transcends time and space and a welcoming attitude towards the beautiful process of aging. Full of life and full of loss with a full acceptance of the inevitability of death. Full of a carefree belief that the circle of life exists.

I question where life will take me. I bounce from project to project with no intentions but to fill the void of stillness. Both blessed and cursed with overflowing opportunities and an abundance of different directions and paths, I surrender to my passions and to my talent. Let me dip my feet into every rapidly flowing river. Let me be swept away by passions and sucked under into chaotic waters only to come up gasping for air when I then float onto my next exhilarating adventure. Let the current guide me.

Let me be careless.

My empty soul once believed, without a doubt, that I was unworthy of the gift of life and love. I was incapable of living a functional life and numb to love both towards myself and others. I could not share a dark and defeated spirit or heart. The blackout within my soul could barely be lit with a dim flicker of hope but it was, and I have slowly continued to fuel the flame and now the fire within me blazes with sparks of life that snap, crackle, and pop into the abyss of darkness where my path explodes and then naturally fades into the unknown of tomorrow.

I've tumbled over rocky paths and fallen off cliffs into raging waters where I fought to breathe only to be washed ashore onto a deserted island where I reside alone with my fear, pain, trauma, and insanity. I never waved or screamed for help. I was never rescued. I slowly pieced together a boat that would take me out into ocean storms where hungry sharks circled, and waves crashed. I fought to find a land grounded with connection, love, and freedom. I searched for meaning in the horizon. I gave up. I waved and screamed for help and the wind picked up.

I am a free spirit and embrace going with the flow and taking direction compliantly. I am stubborn and my compliance at times comes from a place of pleasing instead of personal wants and needs. I now allow the pressure from the strong breeze of support to guide me while also remaining rooted in my freedom of beliefs and desires. The Earth's dirt surrounds my tangled network of staggered past paths and as I rock in the wind, I remain grounded and as my roots reach for the center of the Earth where a tangible reality lives, my branches reach for the stars and my leafy dreams dance to the music of nature.

Life and love now come naturally.

As I hit a sturdy wall standing in the present where I feel complete, I punch through the gray paint which with my stubborn and persistent strength, begins to crack and open into a small, messy hole which when peered through, gives me a vision of a future full of color and abstract patterns that continue to move away from me in this new and expanding room. My hand is cut and bruised, and I want so badly to rip down the entire wall standing between me and my dreams, but I remain stuck in my mind where I am only shown a glimpse.

My undying hope and belief in myself keep me from turning my back and returning to the many rooms in my past where the doors remain open. My strong desire to ask for help is masked by the insecurity of my ideas and my selfish attitude of wanting to reach the future on my own after feeling that I've already made it this far. It is not the unknown of what this untouchable room will offer that scares me; it is the fear that it is yet another delusion. That this space wasn't meant to be shared.

As I continue to get caught and tangled in webs of fear that reside in my current room, I look for inspiration within myself where I am reminded that it is possible to clean and clear out dark, sticky corners of rooms crawling with spiders. The rooms of my past where I sat alone in defeated, foggy corners, now shine with clarity. I will no longer let the spiders of life hold me back. I will not give up. I will rip through the webs but am waiting for the tornado to brew.

I believe it will.

I have been shaped by a life full of love and adventure and as my story continues to unfold, my narration of it is shifting. My ego no longer finds validation in sharing the ebb and flow of experience that became a vicious cycle of defeat, grief, and healing with sprinkles of stability and joy. I now pull the messages learned from my past in hopes of sharing a universal perspective instead of a crazed personal story full of humility that once defined me. My definition of self now encompasses my core values and a purpose that hopes to expose the vulnerability, truth, and wisdom we all possess.

After many times of piecing together my building blocks of life into a new and unique structure, and after repetitively hammering the constructions to tiny shards of waste only to be delicately glued back together where even a soft breeze could crumble the foundation, I am now meticulously and cautiously building a castle which is expanding in strength and durability. A castle guarded by gates that only open for loving family, friends, and mentors who I invite to accompany me on my journey.

After locking myself into closet after closet where I was attacked and tortured by dark monsters and ghosts, I found a key that unlocked a door that opened to a field of dreams where mystical and benevolent creatures grazed calmly and waited for my approach. This expansive and magical room still fills me with fear, but I now confront the unknown of reactions with acceptance and patience. I expose my own vulnerability, truth, and wisdom in hopes of receiving the same.

Which door should I unlock next?

With the death of pity and victimization, which was killed from my beginning, I take ownership for the moments in life that have triggered a spiral of uncontrollable instability. I trust easily and am stubborn about that belief that my intuition is true and should be trusted. I love deeply and am confident about the belief that my feelings are true and should be returned. I suppose I have a sense of narcissism about the belief that who I choose to give my heart to would be the luckiest and that I deserve reciprocation of such love. I suppose these beliefs stem from my skewed idea of love inspired by my first love; a saga that encompassed an overwhelming spectrum of emotions and as a vulnerable and impressionable teenager, defined my expectations of all future loves.

I am waiting for my life story of love, loss, and heartache to come full circle and wash over me with peace and satisfaction with a last love that is both ordinary and extraordinary. I will not search in desperation. I will not settle. I will not lose hope.

Wonderful people are falling into my lap rapidly as I exude positivity, acceptance and maintain an open mentality of no judgement, curiosity, and a kind and cautious idea that we all possess some form of goodness. The options are expanding while I am also aware that I can't assume I have choices. I will search for reciprocity. I will settle for nothing less than a best friend and connection that continues forever to bring color to my face and racing beats to my heart. I will lose myself to passion and daydreams. I will wait.

But where is he? Where is my last love?

I am amid yet another sacred experience; a new and different episode; a moment in time where life feels to have aligned with an energy that inspires my creativity and a willingness to open my heart once again to the unknown. As my life feels to be coming full circle after seventeen years of searching and with a journey towards self-discovery that is still unfolding, I feel somewhat safer to come up for air and breathe in my blessings.

I have been mindfully preparing for life and all its blessings since age seventeen. I try to remain sensitive to the fear that may present in the unprepared without if life will unfold how I want it to or that those I want surrounding me will be willing. I can't help but believe that the gift I have become has transcended into the most beautiful gift for me to now receive. Every single connection my life has given me is a gift and I want to honor all who have guided me.

I need to remind myself that the unknown of the future exists. Those expectations are dangerous. Although the grass is already greener, winter will inevitably come again. That cautious and quiet action speaks louder than an impulsive sprint towards the finish line. That no matter what, I am already a winner.

Let life cheer.

By leaving behind jealousy, resentment fades and understanding and self-compassion grow. Take a healthy dose of selfishness and don't be affected by external matters. Trust yourself and trust that your staggered path will unwind into clear dreams that intersect with all we are connected to and tell the life story we were meant to live.

As comparison fades, balance enters by an ability to look inwards and separate one's needs from others. Finding passion, drive, and competition within myself and striving towards goals from a place of self-worth and a desire for fulfillment, and with an acceptance of past failures and preparation for future ones, I eagerly launch myself forward knowing my niche in life will come with patience, dedication, and hard work.

My dreams are big, but my awareness of false hope and unrealistic expectations is now deeply rooted within my mind. A mind that loves getting lost in the clouds and escaping into a fantasy world where a deep and magical love resides. A stubborn mind once tortured and now resting peacefully in a strong, healthy body. An insane mind still curious and searching for miracles. My mind.

Are you there? Can you hear me?

As my spontaneity gets caught between overlapping clouds where the sky's breeze pushes it with force, where the squeeze then releases and opens into a calm blue space where the overwhelming fears of pressure then relax, I feel balance in the weather. My intense push towards the sun finds a discipline to slow the pace in fear of burning. I find a soft, comfortable seat on a cloud that holds me in stillness while still shifting shapes and directions.

As I sit in patience watching the sun fall, I slowly begin to light up with bright beautiful colors that then fade into a night where I see the moon rise and shooting stars which in their great distance, seem within reach. I lay my head back to rest on a pillow full of fluffy dreams.

I awake to birds soaring past my solid body mass where I remain untouched and undistracted. I find peace in stillness and an awareness in my lack of invincibility, of my fragility and human nature. I close my eyes to the sun and allow the light and heat to kiss my sensitive skin softly.

The kiss makes me blush.

As I dig deeper and deeper, I continue to uncover the root causes of my core issues and as I dive inwards towards the nucleus of my mind where electricity once shocked me into pain, numbness and a tortured ghost who had lost the ability to remain grounded, I now hold firmly onto a strong and steady body. Once weak, withering and with uncontrollable and debilitating tremors, I now embody fully a strict regime of health, fitness and self-care which has brought me strength, structure, accountability, and fulfillment that comes easily.

Life should not always be a battle that brings us to our knees so that we feel the need to cry out and pray for help and freedom. I surrender and live life with ease. I am content and I am buried in hope, inspiration and love that is heavy with passion, that I locked into a box deep within me which even Pandora cannot crack open.

With patience, dedication, and hard work, I have hopes that the time will come when I shovel and unbury this box and release my work and knowledge to share with the world. Or at least I will try to dig deeper and deeper where my box is sharply struck by a magnetic metal that clinks with the luck of life, like a bracelet full of charms.

I clasp this delicate chain carefully around my wrist where symbols of hopes and dreams dangle with grace.

Creativity has led me to an inspiration which manifested unknowns and has made me question reality by showing me different perspectives of life's mysteries. After an exhausting and long search for all possible avenues of reasons for perceiving the impossible and a thrilling and persistent desire to keep returning to this insane research of self-discovery, I finally hit a bottom that I could no longer bounce back from. My obsession lived on in a defeated and numb mind and body which exuded misery and woke me up morning after morning with a fight to go on while believing this was it. That would be my life. That I would never have love, connection or ever fulfill my destiny. But a small flicker of hope continued to burn deep within my vacant and lifeless soul.

I now embody a balanced feeling of love, connection and insanity that is driving me forward with a passion to dream once again. An insanity I have learned to control by honing and directing this spontaneous and once sporadic energy towards sharp, mindful outlets that bring me health and joy. An insanity I now have no shame embracing. An insanity I now want to share with the world while holding onto an awareness of the delusions and torture I have lost myself to in the past.

My mind comes alive each morning as a blank slate full of oblivion yet swimming with curiosity and excitement, and as my day begins, it unfolds with no expectations as my exploration for fulfillment swarms onto my mind's canvas and creates yet a new, colorful, and different abstract perspective. Let me be free to express. Let me share. Let me not be judged.

Let me be crazy.

As my heart pounds with vigor, my lungs catch on to the hot humid air that I suck in with force and my loose mouth pushes out a loud breath that brings my eyes back into a sharp focus and is surrounded by a drooping and brightly flushed face. As my skin dampens and the hair on my arms stands, the muscles in my leg spasm and with the need to collapse, I keep going.

After a quick spin into a perfected position, the ball is placed delicately and with purpose in a corner where I stand alone. Pressure places my nerves into a deep focus; a comfortable place that thrives with expectation and an exhilarating excitement that looks to impress. I make the ball bend effortlessly where it finds another home in a different corner. I remain strong and sturdy as the net shakes.

The crowd rise from their seats, emptying the bleachers and bringing cheers that echo through the stadium where the dispersed players then race towards each other with a thrill that is unforgettable. My exhaustion is forgotten as my strong legs prance with pride back into position as, yet another whistle begins a new chapter of the game.

I've scored in life.

I stand firmly on a ground that overwhelms me with my own perspectives that I won't allow myself to be stripped from my strong grasp onto the Earth. I pace steadily in circles as I look for a middle ground that holds me steady and where my autonomy and independence will not get lost in a frenzy of controlling opinions that once defined my path. I should be free to have a say. To be heard and understood. To stay honest, stand up for myself and speak to disagreements. I should be in the driver's seat cruising towards my own desires.

I have not always known what is best for me and give my undying gratitude to those who have guided me towards a life direction that is now accelerating with purpose, and a mission to remain focused and sharp as my engine continues to pick up, and I race between the lines with no competition and with the hope of crossing the finish line unscathed.

As I continue to update my vehicle while looking to be carried both safely and with power, I remain calmly and patiently in the back seat where I get lost in the lives and structures that pass me and move me closer to my destination. I see the reflection of my eyes in the rearview mirror for just a moment and then my gaze finds rest on the path ahead.

Hand over the keys.

A once vulnerable heart that would easily shatter into fragments of chaotic, sharp reactions and heartache now repels the bullets of rejection and attacks with a new and now overconfident anger that intimidates and believes to know what is felt and needed with an arrogant perspective that feels deserving of love. I believe the power of love and the magic it inspires and creates can only be possible when both parties have equally surrendered to the magnetic energy, temptation, desire and even obsession and desperation that ignites the miracles within us and our higher powers. Maybe I have once again released a ghost to roam a delusional world of love where it resides alone in its search for meaning. Maybe it's time for me to surrender to a truth I will not open my eyes to. But my intuition tells me I know best.

Love and joy can manifest in many forms, and I no longer fear dying alone or without a loving companion. But the love I fantasize about and seek in life is a rare and powerful one which although unrealistic, keeps me from settling into a committed and safe partnership where I would still find happiness. My heart has not yet aligned into a satisfaction of feeling complete equality, comfort, and safety with love. When given, my heart has not been received. When gifted, my uncertain heart declines.

Life and love are not always fair, balanced, or mutual. There is compromise, sacrifice and there is uncertainty. There are disagreements and there are concerns. There are fears. Let me love fearlessly and let me be loved. Let my heart be stupid. Let my heart be solid and let my mind melt. Let the force of love find me and let me not force. Let my youthful dreams come alive. Let love triumph.

Let it be.

I've climbed the Rocky Mountains only to slip and fall back into a cave of oblivion where a scary darkness haunts me with delusions of evil shadows and demons. I fought to maintain equality and haunted this darkness in return with a kindness, love and light that kept me alive as I continued to pull my heavy body upwards towards clouds that emulated visions of gods and goddesses seen with a vividness, I knew were for my insane eyes only.

As the mountain snow melts and the icy water flows downwards where it falls and crashes into a freezing body of blood that I once would drown in, I grab a tight hold of warm, dry stone, sun kissed with a hope that pulls me out of the melting pot of a now bubbling and boiling red lava waiting to explode into the universe where its ash works its way through cracked clouds and lands on the sun.

I welcome and confront my fear of great heights with a pursuit to continue challenging myself and push my capabilities to the limits, so I continue to become surprised, like a rainbow continues to shine color on my black and white and all or nothing mindset. As the skies become gray and gloomy, I remain safe in a heaven where I look down and see my countless blessings in falling rain drops.

Tears of joy fall from grace.

The remodel of my home is coming to an end as the once weak foundation has been torn to the ground and rebuilt into a sturdy and stable structure where I find comfort in my favorite room, where I feed a fire that keeps me warm and cozy. The smoke rises into a chimney that shoots high into a sky that fills with dream containing clouds which then disperse and disappear into open, clean air which clears my words and worries. I sip on hot tea that steams floral smells of blooming hopes into the safety of the enclosed room filled with unread books which I let sit and build with dust. Shelves remain open.

The television sings to my inviting ears and my computer shows words unfolding into reflections of a soul that sits behind penetrating eyes. My fingers feel a keyboard that mindlessly clicks to the rhythm of a free heart which in its thoughtless vomit of words, finds passion in a creative outlet that has transferred from the secrets of diaries containing scribbles of childhood dramas and doodles of initialed hearts. I find a youthful and carefree method of expression as I continue to write.

I look to the bookshelves where lost memories reside inside ends that keep them tightly pushed together in their masses and do not yet feel it is time to return to the past. I will wait for the library to be complete. I will wait for the stories to choose when to unfold and open to pages both ripped and burnt as well as clean and crisp. I will wait to climb to the top shelf where I'll eventually read and learn the dictionaries of languages I never understood. I will wait patiently.

I will find the words.

As I scrape away the layers from the old paintings I had locked deep within the closet of my heart, the dry and damaged acrylics flake off and dance weightlessly to the floor. The canvases reveal bits and parts of an abstract love that awakens lost and vulnerable memories which I had continuously covered and avoided with new creations.

I am finally ready to keep peeling away these past distorted fantasies and greet the future with a fresh paintbrush which will manifest a new love that is here to stay and will be hung on an empty wall which waits, to be admired at once life naturally progresses with new and different experiences that paint my life with colorful memories.

I want to remember a life with fleeting regrets and as I pull out a blank canvas, I acknowledge that this too may be painted over during a process of inevitable grief until I am once again ready to chip away at the pain and start fresh. For now, though, I express myself with confidence and a persistence that moves freely with the flexibility of a paint brush, as well as sharply with a meticulous drawing where the pencil used never dulls.

Let my mind be blown with creativity.

Over a lifetime, a huge array of people will weave themselves throughout; all of whom touch us in some way even if they only have a small impact during a moment. There are the people we choose to keep in our lives, and who keep us in theirs, and these connections should be carefully chosen. These are the forever people in our lives who, over time, grow to become people who receive and give a deep unconditional love and support. These are people who will care for you when you are ill or at your bottom and people who will lift you up and cheer you on while you are thriving. These are people who will never drag you down from the pursuit of fulfilling your dreams. These people are your equals.

There are the first and only dates, the strangers you stay up with all night in deep conversation and those you share a smile with and greet on the street. They have all touched and moved me even in the slightest way. They all have become a part of my life network and story. They have all given me a small flash of memory that pushes me to continue my journey towards curiosity and my search for meaning and inspiration. They are all scattered throughout my twisted path and as they continue to move in and out of my life and as my path straightens, it becomes clear who I am choosing, wisely, to remain with me on this journey.

My lifelong friendships and unavoidable family relationships who once swayed me with their knowledge and opinions no longer influence my insecurity of intelligence and I now embrace my own perspectives, decisions, and choices. My once withered confidence and lack of self-worth due to feeling ostracized and alone, are now thriving with pride for my differences. With an open mind and a full heart, I share my own thoughts and opinions kindly without expecting or even wanting an agreeable response. This is my story. My life.

Who are you?

I live each day with the intention of jumping onto the most direct route towards instant gratification and the embodiment of fast paced productivity and growth. I am beginning to find mastery of doing so without stress or pressure and what I once fought so hard to accomplish I have now committed to with a graceful and easy motivation. A motivation that brings structure to my life and an accountability that is holding me tightly in the present. A present place of peace and satisfaction that I want to hold onto so badly.

I don't want to be disappointed. I don't want to lose everything, feel failure, and once again start my life all over from a place of emptiness and loss. I have hopes and desires and will act with caution as I live each day moving closer to dreams that I won't allow to crumble to the ground.

I've had past dreams of writing a novel or many and could never commit to focus on such a lengthy story which made sense and came full circle. I could not find patience to do so and so my dreams have shifted to a realistic form of creatively expressing myself through writing. As I quickly jot my reflections down each day, I receive the instant gratification I seek. I learned something new. I complete something. It is fun and it is rewarding. But I still want to be an author of some form of book or many.

So, I write.

As wisdom blooms from the depth of my life experiences, my once foggy path is becoming clear and my decisions which once were stupid and dangerous are now engrained with caution and care. By learning the hard way that choices made may have a deep and meaningful effect on myself and others, and now having knowledge and a healthy fear of the pain these choices once resulted in, my sprint and impulsivity towards success and accomplishments now have slowed to peaceful waves and a calm breeze of wisdom.

From inspiration ignited by love, hope, and gratitude, I gracefully weave through discomfort, disappointment and hurt with balance, acceptance, and an openness to bravery as well as a discovery of pride. A pride that once was a motivator towards fame and fortune has now become a slowly burning and growing appreciation of small steps forward.

A seemingly insignificant improvement now glows from within my once unsatisfied spirit. The spark in my eyes that shines outwards and settles on the eyes of others lights a fire within my soul with the intention of projecting a reflection of miraculous effect onto those who I find genuine, real, and fascinating.

Am I fascinating? That is the greatest compliment of all.

Whether it is a harsh storm or beating sun rays, an umbrella hovers above my small yet growing mind serving as protection and as I gaze down objectively from above, I see a full life overflowing with impactful, powerful events and connections; both magnificent and torturous. I am detached yet fully own my story and as a slight breeze blow, I look up to check the weather only to be reminded that I can't see or expect whether the skies will roar or peacefully glow or not.

I hear a song and my eyes shuffle back in time to look down and land on that one wild and free night in high school. A pure memory of complete innocence and joy makes my heart sink and clouds accumulate and as the grief and loss of invincibility and blissful ignorance pour down and drip onto my shoes where they fade slowly, so do my tears. I step forward dry and unscathed.

I stumble upon a photo and my heart expands into my chest where pressure rests and a storm of passion brews. A growing light from above creates a shadow of different objects that surround me and as I move freely into bright spaces, new territory is marked with yet another unique silhouette.

Life is puzzling. Am I missing a piece?

Bees buzz through the meadow of my mind whispering in a language I try to understand yet know I am only retaining bits and pieces of the messages meant to guide me back to my hive. A place of teamwork. As I ignore the swarm's movement towards a home whose busy society has expectations of set accomplishments I don't want to follow, I fly alone towards lonely desires which give me a selfish thrill of rebellion.

I beat my wings to my own rhythm in search of the most poisonous pollen where I look to risk the fight for survival even if it means I get sick along my journey. If I take my own path towards becoming strong and resilient enough to level up to queen, I will take the path less travelled. I want to have my freedom.

I want to be my own leader without authority hovering, while deeply understanding that teamwork is important and listening to all perspectives with an open, accepting, and nonjudgmental mind while maintaining my own opinions is what will inspire others and attract fellow bees to help me make the sweetest honey. A honey that although may take more work to manifest, will be worth the wait.

It will feed my hunger.

I was asked and I am asking myself to reflect on my internal perceptions of how my impulsive thoughts transcended into a temporary discomfort which questioned my future actions. My stubborn and obsessive character never gives up without a fight as my mind battles eagerly between right and wrong; good and bad. As my soul screams for freedom, my heart yearns for comfort and as my hand reaches for the glass of wine, I remind myself to think. What are the consequences?

By allowing a sip, I am free, and I am comforted yet *my* truth is no longer *the* truth as I slip back into a web of lies. It is the negative internal perceptions of my self-worth and honesty that consume my misery and leave me alone and imprisoned. There is not *my* truth. *The* truth sets me free yet by protecting all I love, including myself, I diminish pain and fear with a smile. It becomes clear that my definition of freedom was skewed. Freedom cannot be faked. Freedom becomes free only by surrendering.

As my heart and mind find a balanced freedom between love and wisdom, I walk freely and safely forward into an unknown with confidence of my ability to utilize the tools once overshadowed by impulsivity. Let me act on love with caution. Let me act on wisdom with compassion. Let me surrender with patience and trust the universe to act with me.

I was asked and I am asking myself. Let's act.

My daily walk steps my one-track mind forward and the familiarity of the dirt path surrounded by trees and water gives me an anticipation of the clearing where the bridge comes into view. A bridge that represents the transition from nature to city. A bridge that crosses open water where kayaks roam beneath, and bats wait under. Bats that congregate in masses where they hang hidden inside the structure, only to release chaotically all at one into the falling sun which signals their nightly expeditions. My daily walks may not show me them, but I know they are close.

As I reach the stairs leading up to the bridge, my goal-oriented mind again finds a small sense of accomplishment in what the bridge signifies. Although just a minor milestone, the repetition within my days still finds a structure that moves me across boundaries and keeps my one-track mind directed towards a fast-paced place that each day, I prepare to reach. If only my tracks could be remembered.

My continual preparation for my solo expedition towards a bustling place full of new and unique faces remains at a pace which keeps my legs steady, my gaze undistracted and my spirit unaffected. My mission and purpose in life may be clouded as are the tops of tall buildings, but my commitment to open the door and climb the stairs where I am shown a view never seen before, motivates a lack of fear. What I do know is that my tracks leading up to an open and unknown sky are not alone. The footsteps may be at first muddy, but as I continue to work my way upwards, the staircase becomes clean and clear.

I step with precision.

I will fall asleep to my own mind's celebrations of an accomplished year and will wake to different numbers on a constantly changing watch that I had set with the intention of doing so again next year. I will live each day as my last while remaining safe, avoiding the danger of my impulsive mind, and hoping the next 365 days will be lived to the fullest while I consistently tick forward as well as jolt with anticipation of the alarms of life.

The clock of my biology speeds up to the fear that what I am waiting for will enter my life too late. That my choice to hold out for a kiss that will find me every day of each year for the rest of my life adds unnecessary pressure to the air between my lips and theirs. That the desperation I deny exists is deeply rooted in my desire to share my journey as one with another.

As the clock continues to tick, I get closer to the regrets of chances missed. I also speed up to myself and to my dreams. If only I could turn the knob counterclockwise. If only I could set my alarm to what is destined. If only time stood still in my fantasies. But I will feel closely the present time guides me forward and will only set the timer when needed. For now, I will put my watch away.

What time is it?

If we have a passion and dream to be a ballerina, yet it is not within our gifts or talents to be so, we must find acceptance that our fantasy of finding stardom on a stage full of grace, beauty and flexibility will still be felt and shared in the emotions inspired. Let those who do possess the talents gifted to them in their lucky destiny of limber dance share their passionate souls and bend in gratitude to a desire to become a small part of the experience. Let yourself witness a moving performance from the audience even though the light that shines within the theatre is not falling on you.

I must surrender to my fight to become the best at everything I do just because maybe I can. I must stop fighting my true passions, gifts and talents that are finding me with an ease that allows for a stress free and fulfilling life. I must remove the pads wrapped around my bruised and blistered feet that once sprinted away from my true passion of creativity towards the high expectations of myself that believed I was scoring in life because I could. My feet are tired.

Let my feet bruise and blister in fashionable shoes that walk me briskly towards my destiny and passions. Let me kick up the puddles and carelessly dirty the materials of life. Let me wash away life's worries by surrendering to a freedom that in my blind avoidance, has been right in front of me all along. Let me paint my heart in colorful words.

Let me speak to my passions.

My drive was disrupted by a tap on the window and my bleeding heart exchanged two quarters for a small and flimsy newspaper. A newspaper we in Seattle knew could be found on street corners and under bridges. A few cents well earned by the dirtied and desperate man. My car sat beneath a bridge – a place I had sat many times before with the anticipation of the extremely long wait for a green light which would signal my speed forward and leave behind this man along with my memory of his service. Instead, I witnessed something beautiful unfold as one act of kindness carried on.

As my eyes found the rearview mirror and saw the man approach the car behind, my focus found the hand of the passenger reaching out with two quarters. The driver received his newspaper and my rush to push my foot to the pedal eased me to a hope of remaining put. The windows continued to domino down as the newspapers thinned in the hands of the spirited and ragged man who graciously collected his payments and moved onto the next.

The goodness was contagious and melted my heart into a pool of hope that was a reminder of the power of passing it on. I couldn't help but believe those witnessing the effect of each act of generosity were excited for their turn to share and become a part of the lineage. The man's hands became full of quarters and empty of newspapers. I assumed the cars who missed their chance of partaking were saddened. I saw smiles build behind me and as the light turned green, I drove off slowly into a place that wasn't so distant from the swelling in my heart.

Goodness does exist.

The ebb and flow of inspiration continues to brush the sea glass clean only to push them further from the wave I am riding. As the glass becomes small and its edges smooth, the sharpness of my big dreams slowly begins to fade into grains of sand that teeter on an edge between calm dry beach and crashing waves. What once contained a message, now contains the beauty of transformation. What was once trash, is now treasure.

The sea glass continues to change, and the once translucent bottle has been broken and molded into small opaque shapes that no longer piece together to complete the puzzle. I collect the dispersed pieces that originated from all of what contained my cries for help and place them in a jar where they sit in a beautiful array of colors and tell my broken life story. They tell me my path can be scattered and still come full circle where I am able to choose the parts I want to remember and hold onto. I see a jar waiting to become full.

First, I must return to the wet sand where I dip my toes into inspiration. The waves no longer crash around me and pull my body under where life is sucked from my already empty soul. I no longer choose the waters of self-sabotage. I am now cautiously creating footprints in wet sand which despite washing away along with my expectations, remain consistent and continue to stumble upon sea glass that will complete a jar that remains half full. As bottles continue to fill the waters, my patience finds satisfaction in the wait for transformation.

I surrender to the messages.

The broken and chipped wood fence contains wild horses with an idea of boundaries. Seen with an instinctive eye, the horses knew they were meant to stay together in this confined space even though they still had the choice to easily break through into vast fields where their wildness could freely buck into the sunset. They could be free to explore a land that offered flowing streams full of life and greenery which would surround them expansively. Instead, they remain in the safety of this slotted space that sits by a busy road where cars speed by with passengers who turn their heads in carelessness at the trapped horses who graze sadly in their imprisonment. An imprisonment we all are trapped in.

The playground symbolizes a slot of time for breath and although it maintains structure and allows for physical play and exercise for the students throughout a tightly scheduled day, it also teases them with an idea that the choice is not theirs when they feel the need for a break. When they feel overwhelmed from the pressures of school or home life, they should be in touch with those triggers and have an awareness of the need to find release. When the need to release stress is monitored, the feelings will inevitably build and be expressed in other forms.

The wildness within us may feel the need to rebel but we are not always capable of keeping ourselves safe and those who are blind to the fence that does so, may wander off and break through into a life that potentially brings danger and hardships. Or maybe we grow and discover something extraordinary that the path least travelled offers. Maybe we gain original wisdom that only those who wander gain. Just maybe our desire and curiosity to explore the unknowns beyond the fence will guide us towards a deeper discovery of self. Maybe our support cautiously lets the fence become broken and chipped allowing us choice. The fences of our lives may sway in the wind or crumble to the ground but no matter what, we should embrace the spaces we choose to explore.

Where will my wildness wander next?

I feel safe and grounded in a new fantasy that pulls my energy deep into the abyss of a mind, body and soul that remains stable and realistic as it gets lost in dreams which begin to solidify and where I continue to find inspiration and a higher power in my mind's creativity. Even though my mind's trickery still lingers, I am aware and accept that I may never believe my experiences were pure delusion. I can't help but believe one experience and vision was felt and seen and began my journey towards the moon.

My vulnerable mind is scared to admit in its insanity that I believe I've been elsewhere where I was shown miracles. That the power of creativity has guided me safely through a colorful ocean of both intense light and darkness where I would rise into a mysterious horizon where I would be released from my imprisonment to explore the universe freely.

I no longer need validation or proof of the impossible. I own my mind and can now admit to the craziness of my persistent search for affirmation. I may be alone behind my sparkling eyes that see a world of color and a life of love, but I am no longer scared of my mind's isolation. I no longer feel the need to expose my deepest secrets that I tried so hard to share in hopes of an approval that validated something I now know is my experience only. I no longer feel held down by the strong current of judgment and concern.

I will fly higher.

———

Creep into the pain. Suck the life out and pull the vampire within me into the shining daylight where I crackle and harden. Let me shed yet another layer of reality and share a piece of truth in hope of giving a piece of light for you too. A kind of light stemming from my heart's truth with a desire to crack the rock in the core of your ignorance. A light that comes only from love that beams like the shrills and shrieks of pain which came from my widened and sad mouth in my past. The pain that has stuck with you and left you as you are now. Is it my fault? Let me help. It's now my turn to help.

I'm hungry and tired of chasing what doesn't want to be caught. I'm tired of tiptoeing around in the dark and getting messy. The sun always rises, and they will have to confront the issues they have fought so hard to avoid. As much as I tell myself I am strong and have a voice – I will never feel that I am not a child or cannot be in trouble. I do not feel like an adult or that I have a choice. Perhaps my circumstances are proof of that.

Escaping into the night sounds somewhat magical now. At least then, I am different, and I am free. I may not be an adult, but I am something. Something else. Something on my own. Let me run wild through my imagination into the dark woods where I hunt for my own food only because that's what we need to do for survival – not by choice. Let me find love and I know I would in this life since it would be eternal. Let me dream since mine keep being torn away.

Let me wake up, too.

No need to call me by name since it is unknown by even me. I do not trust those who left me one. Yet I cannot help but leave my heart with them. I do not recognize the person I was – the one with no name. I feel as if I have been recognized by many names and am now today settled and maintaining one. Fast forward – changes occur, and I may not recognize myself as I now do not recognize them. I reflect on this now, as this deeply saddens me, and my hope is to maintain inner beauty and value. I want to keep my last given name. The one I worked for.

What I work for is what is my calling. Call me Rebecca – my given name. I take pride in everything I do – and I work hard while taking the most direct route in all pursuits. While doing so, I've had success, failure and learned different shortcuts towards avenues that would allow for other ventures. I jump full force into projects allowing for many talents to be utilized and tested. What will I most excel at in life?

As I propel forward into what seems like a never-ending unknown of dreadful monotony – I also have a spark of peace knowing life feels like it is finally coming full circle in the sense that I am finding satisfaction in my community, my general satisfaction with life and most importantly my mind. Even though there are some key factors absent that would add to my quality of life – I can only look to patience and hope while I find gratitude in what I currently obtain. As of now, you know me a little better.

Call me Becca.

The collision strikes the core of my soul where the light withheld then explodes and accelerates uncontrollably into a magical place where love and dreams reside. Sharp messages are seen with intention and understood as guidance towards a star that after fighting rigorously to reach it, now seems approachable. I surrender to the forceful pace that moves me forward towards the shining light that continues to brighten while grasping the reins tightly. I gallop into the unknown.

I prance into his open arms – fully embraced and accepted. I am safe now. My heart has traveled near and far – it has been lost in deep, dark ocean waters where sharks circled, and it has drifted far into the universe only to be consumed by black holes. My heart has felt pain and it has felt fear. My heart, though, has loved. It has never, though, been in a home as it is today.

The pressure in my chest whispers a love song softly, meant as a hopeful secret – I must protect the fragility. This is too much, yet this is all I've asked for. I will embrace and accept my blessings as those have embraced and accepted me. I will inspire and be inspired. I will end the battle that has kept me contained and I will open my soul and float on.

I will just be.

As the mist in the jungle rises, I begin to piece together the letters that I couldn't find to complete even the simplest words in my fogged and tangled mind. I was lost in the confusion and chaos of senseless sentences and incomplete hearts. I was running through the fog into a jungle where I was lost in others' uncertainties that seemed too big for my small worries to take to heart. My head is full of quicksand – I alone walk the plank – repeatedly. I fall and sink slowly.

Yet here I am again. Hopeful, excited and with an open heart – I will always be the one to walk the plank, proudly. Walk all over me and inspire me with your pity. Better yet, let me blow your mind with unexpected growth, progress, and fulfillment. In some ways – I believe it's all deeply expected. Of course, it is. I stand blindfolded at the edge of the plank – I don't know whether to fall or jump. I have never jumped.

I find the words to tear through the jungle of life that has held my mind captive and my heart lonesome. I find the ship in my heart sailing my soul to freedom and reminding me of the tangled world I cannot control or calm and remember all is meant to be. I find myself on the plank of this ship screaming for freedom and not only jumping but leaping into the quicksand of my mind. How deep can I go? At times, I want to disappear.

This time – I want to break through to the other side.

Tumbling over tombstones and sprinting over pinecones – I piece together jagged pineapples in this strange puzzle where I justify that I still have the talent and capability within my withering and slowing mind, to find the shapes to complete the masterpiece. I collect the details of my life and see them for what they are and have them come to fruition – come full circle and explode into a reality that is touchable to only me. I alone complete the puzzle.

I alone compete. I run wild alone in deluded places where monsters trick me into creeping down staircases leading to crashing waves and spiky rocks. I alone sneak through the cracks of the threads in my pillowcase into the depths of my dreams where I am haunted, to believe I will win in life. I reside alone in this wishful space that protects my mind from torture. Without the torture, I wouldn't see the beauty.

I see beauty. I see beauty in the tombstones. The light in her eyes can't be shed by the tears shown – she knows she is beautiful. The darkness in the world can't be brighter just because. Light always prevails. Love always shines for the darkness to see. Impact stands alone. Inspiration stems from love and loss. Beauty can't be proved.

Prove them wrong.

Life can be rocky, and full too. I have found myself beaten to a pulp by those I admire most while telling myself I am never good enough. I am torn apart only to be reminded once again of my weaknesses. I also dance to my own pride, sing to the moon, swim under the stars, and love this life I live so much I would never change it for another. I love my family and I love my friends and all the people who have been brought into my life, who have moved me and shared their wisdom.

It's the wisdom that killed me. There is so much darkness in this world. The explosion of fascination and curiosity that consumed me at such a young age was nothing less than pure danger. I can't help but believe, here I am today – wiser, and here to share some messages I've learned – silly, or not. And it's not because others can't. I want to.

I will spend my entire life exploring what it is I hope to shed light on. I want to crack open just one capsule of untouched ideas and create an explosion of excitement within a network and get thoughts moving in all directions. I think big, but why not? For now, my patience sits deep while my focus remains on my wellness.

It's a bit rocky.

My wishful leaps of hope keep me grasping for air in this suffocating room that keeps my dreams far from safe. I am terrified. I am surrounded yet never more alone. I am sad. My insides explode into an uncontrolled abyss where chaos shoots in all directions and anxiety induces all only to suck back in and darken my entire being with all that exists. Help.

But there is hope, as always. There is perspective and there is tomorrow. All is temporary and I know a bright future lies ahead. A wave of discomfort washes over the speck of story in my life and I hold tightly onto something new. Not my family this time. My mind is screaming. Maybe they will take me back.

I am a true peacemaker at heart and have high hopes of making amends while also knowing the pain is buried deep and may never be unrooted if the work is not done. That is in their hands. To me, they have held the universe in their hands. That is possibly what makes this all so sad.

Yet acceptable.

My hope is to find purpose in inspiration. An inspiration which stems from a love that shines light into words, that transcends the fog during my mind. My struggle to find the words reflects my struggle to find love. Where is he? As my search for purpose continues, my beating heart sinks deeper into patience. I am inspired since I am self-loving. But who loves me?

I move gracefully through this tangled life knowing I will once again be guided towards peace of mind and satisfaction. I sit up and feel alive, inspired, and loved. I feel inspiration boiling in my blood. I feel it tingling on my skin and standing in my hair. I may be fragile, but I can also be repaired – which has been proved over and over, again.

I want to have an existence in this universe. I hope to send a message of hope that inspires others to search for their own self-love. As I move through the chaos of the cosmos, I reflect on my journey and piece together all that has brought me to where I am today. My story is far from done.

Inspire me.

SAYINGS:

Part II

You are the color in my soul and the melody in my step. You are my smile, and you are my laugh. You are my soulmate and best friend. You are the dance in my body and the voice in my head. I will love you forever. I will kiss you always. I am yours.

The sky opened as clouds drifted and the full moon illuminated its surroundings just as I had moved towards light from my darkness.

My demons brought me closer to manic moments of late nights and racing thoughts. My energy picked up along with my social impulsiveness. I was running through a maze with no map, hoping I would reach the end by following my heart. My free spirit needed restraint but my wild, stubborn character would not be leashed. I lay in bed with my demons only with the desire to forget them and keep going.

He was the safety net for the secrets that haunted her. Tightly bound by strength and wisdom, he stood sturdy as her past fell into him. Her arms opened with vulnerability and fear as she stepped closer to the ledge. She was caught by love and never felt safer.

The light in the distance was nowhere to be found as I trudged through an ugly moment of dark thoughts and delusional dreams. The vacancy in my eyes saddened the loves of my life as I became stuck in a web of sticky shadows. I yearned for freedom yet fighting became tiresome. My mind was eating me away.

The muse gets lost in the dreamer's imagination just in time for the conception of creative innovation. The muse gifts artistic inspiration while the artist finds freedom in passion of expression. The loving fascination the artist has towards their muse inspires a projection of genius originality. Inventive creativity is fueled by the connection to the mysterious.

Her life's purpose was freedom. Her winding journey had taken her through obstacles that brought bouts of growth. The maturation of self-awareness would continue as she set forth into new beginnings. Exploration was at her fingertips, and she felt blooming openness in her soul.

———

The unlovable wash ashore black sand beaches where upon standing they fall deeply into the wet earth. Their misinterpreted journey sinks them into thoughts of unworthiness. They feel stuck yet move forward with nudges from the water. Waves crash around their knees and push them further from balance. The unlovable reach the hot, dry sand where truth drips from their bodies. They have been smothered by an ocean of love.

Caught by numbness and sinking into herself, she still knew she was not the victim. Brought forth by love and concern, she would find hope in her surroundings. She left behind her demons for a new beginning where her mind's turmoil would be found and healed. Self-destruction was no longer an option as she awoke at peace in a paradise for those who wander.

———

Along with grief comes wisdom and clarity. Heartache may linger but she had accepted her past while having awareness of life's continued turbulence. She had the inner tools to persevere and a soft yet stubborn demeanor that brought forth willingness. Her present confidence left her with a readiness for life.

Her openness to connection and acceptance of differences gave the gift of knowledge that quenched her thirst for the unknowns. She hoped the authenticity of her creative mind would attract the curious and subdue judgments. She remained patient with the present moment while her imagination dreamed of a magical future.

The purity of her youthful essence was being found once again as she expressed honesty and authenticity. Her openness attracted love and acceptance as dwindling connections reformed. She forgave herself and felt present with a new beginning. She radiated an infectious positivity that she prayed would encompass her being forever.

The positive attributes that my youth exuded were coming to life once again. I felt invigorated by my dreams and content with accepting they do not always come true. A tumultuous period had come to an end and a new chapter had begun. I was going to embrace another chance.

My vulnerability left open wounds unhealed and prevented my fragile skin from scarring. At least then, the world could not see the permanence of my pain. The mark on my elbow began the story of when my life was ignited by war and more battle wounds would be had. My scars are a reminder of my past while motivating me towards an exposed and full future.

Her loneliness drew her to a desirable interaction that brought excitement and anticipation to her boredom. She caught herself distracted by daydreams as her mind wandered into an entanglement of blissful thoughts. She felt balance as she breathed and a calmness in her pursuit. Her open heart was inviting and the clarity in her mind was allowing her to love.

———

Music from the guitar enveloped the living area as she sat cross legged on the couch facing the Hawaiian sunset. Her mind felt clear for the rhythm to enter and dance through her core. She felt the evening breeze through the open door and sighed a peaceful breath of gratitude. The strings of the instrument continued to vibrate and heal her brokenness.

I opened my eyes to hazel green grass that stood high and was pushed by love. Bent but not broken, my heart resurrected all feeling. I closed my eyes and saw all the colors and it was no longer a dream.

A blissful pressure in my chest tingles deeply into ecstasy.

———

He fascinates me with a sensitivity and tenderness that transcends the tangible and makes him quiver with my love. He fascinates me with a blissful calmness that settles into his core and ignites me to entertain. He fascinates me with heartfelt movements that melt his blushing face into paleness.

———

Every song listens to me as I listen to the message meant for my survival. Tuned into reality yet struck by insanity, I push at the deepest rhythms of the heart.

The depth of internal chaos and withering passion ignites my already deadened idea of life.

An unbelievable memory of the one who stole me haunts my mind and pushes my body into an unexplainable fear of painful love.

———

The opening moves upward and pauses before an explosion of blackouts and floral visions.

I'm thought to be an old soul, yet I search for newness only possible by a soul never to have lived. My search for the discovery of profound existence continues during this original life.

———

Our clocks tick for tomorrow as you awake ahead of me knowing our hearts tick in unison as my lost hours chase you wherever you go.

My careless past washes away as my body moves with rhythm towards unknown life carried between my two loves.

———

Once gratified by lost hours alone then turned to impulsivity, I now come home again to creative pleasures where time stops peacefully.

My insides ebb and flow, doubting and hoping as my yearning heart patiently stimulates dreams of a growing family with you.

Intuition embodies the fragility of never feeling jealousy shown through compatibility of talents known by all yet felt with depth true only to them.

―――

My detached soul is pushed upward uncontrollably only to be grounded delicately by safe, loving protection.

Stuck between matters of the impossible and synchronized perfections of seen movement lucid to my eyes only, I move into an oblivion of truth.

The pursuit of empathy stalls the contact between the feeling of connection and the desire to be more.

―――

Every song beats deep inside my desperate heart where it withers and blossoms into a synchronized melody of a love story.

My swollen eyes move back and forth as they fall upon blurriness that lightens the space with a delusional perspective.

Free from my insanity, I float through acceptance of my most feared dreams.

———

The game of lies and bribery exhausts my fragility and is overbearing for my neglecting of self-pity.

Married to a madness that once chased me through a maze of lies and deceit, I find myself amid a final push towards now meeting him outside my dreams.

No flower could ever show me if you love me or love me not because each petal will always be plucked into a deeper and more beautiful story of true love.

―――

Every song sings to my detached body and vibrates through my moving mind. Speaking from an impossible assumption, I imagine a world of connection and possibilities where happenings occur from meaning.

Unfolding into misery and rising into bliss, I find comfort in my unknown life.

Overfilling jovial energy embraces the insecurity within my diminishing body soon to become sexy once again and make my hard work rewarding for my anticipation and patience.

My dark space now shoots rays of light into my soul and onto other dimensions.

Every song filled me with a magical tenderness that blossomed into the melody of our love and pushed at the rhythms of my heart.

You fascinated me from an image on a screen and with time you stood before me where my youth flawlessly directed your life and love with no judgment of public perceptions.

Stigma chooses those who fear acceptance of self. Our flaws fear stigma as we journey through preferences and discover if we can be true to our passions. Open and careless, we accept our likes and dislikes with not a worry of judgment. We do not judge those who close their door to acceptance of inner conflict.

I now smile with my eyes after grief and misery. I now love and am loved. I now find passion and hope while alone and scared. I now know I can live just once and feel fulfilled and forever childish. My heart aches and it swells. My heart is forever yours.

―――

Death for me is death for him. When he passes, I will be reborn. Life and death are one and the same.

He fascinates me with selfless motives that push me to freedom following entrapment of mind, body, and soul.

Judgment stems deep within our own insecurities and the acceptance and love we find for ourselves will set us free.

Creative expression led me to a vision that would haunt me with its beauty and push me to question reality. By being shown such impossible vividness, I sought answers through a narrative that gave clarity to my insanity. My mind has not manifested such a vision since and I will forever wonder about the meaning behind this impossible unknown. I can only dream of one day uncovering what I continue to question during my research of the mysteries of the mind.

VIGNETTES:

Part III

———

Altered Between Caring Delights Enveloped Forever, Growing High, Inviting, Jiving. Knowing Light, My Numbness Opens Painlessly; Quivering, Reeling Slowly Towards Upward Visions with Xenial Yearning Zaps.

ANIMALS

Wanting my computer and free without. Escaped and nearly lost by wooded greenery and dirt paths; I breathe again. Opened to found fields where the horse stood sturdy and apple slices disappeared. The spiral, wood staircase led downward towards a rocky beach where our eyes waited on whales. Smokey fireside meals and card games made my hands move through the stiff island air. Take me back and write here with me.

You clench your core and sprint forward towards pounding hearts and raw movement. Your neck aches from outwardly pushing your mind at prey. The chatter within twists your body into a disconnected consortium of feelings known only by you. Pressure moves under your skin, sharpens your senses and mental birth is conceived. You push your tail back and shoot forward with new life.

Their dogs grew older along with the family until they passed along with time. The puppy came as a surprise. She galloped from cushion to cushion, and her sharp teeth matured on our raw skin. Squeaking toys were heard and puddles of pee were found. We will grow older once again and our puppy will as well. She will find our dogs and we will move on to new beginnings.

BRAINS

The bell rang, class was dismissed, and my brain ached from the multiple-choice test. My psychology course drowned me with perspective on the complications of my own mind. I waddled across the icy campus; my ears plugged but not closed to the music that played on repeat. Finding meaning in a few songs surrounded me with closeness to something greater. My brain found rhythm as my pencil had found the test bubbles.

You run wild through your mind's connections with no home but the nucleus of your brain. The electricity of your awakened neurons ignites your fiery roar that reaches other minds. You burrow deeply into hunger and rise scurrying into feeding your tortured wisdom. Explosive synapses catch your chemicals before dying into exhaustion. You awaken to chaos and dwindle into the center and safety of your mind's innards.

Her mind bloomed later in life and opportunity would be at her fingertips. She wore her heart on her sleeve instead of thinking love through. She dozed into dreams between classes and her young heart found stubbornness in fantasy. A time would come when all would melt away; her mind would repress, and she would pull down her sleeves.

CRAZY

The impulsive nature of her persistent character stemmed from youthful past experiences. These crazy events would bring her to a crazier reality. She looked past the grief into hopeful horizons where life could simply be how it was before. Her persistent nature would work impulsively towards crazy dreams that could be a reality.

You glance with purpose and wonder if people know. Your mind is frazzled and your body limps as your eyes open to new perspectives. The magnetic force of united moving parts is set free by released pressure and calmed energy. You find refuge in spaces open to exploration and playfully adapt. The crazed girl within you laughs at the dangerously competitive nature of your mind's trickery. The girl fights for fearful love unknown.

She walked fiercely down the brightly lit runway with the headpiece sitting heavy and fabrics flowing behind.

Blinded by the light with crazed cat-eye makeup, she reminded herself of the piercing glance given to impress. Posing and turning at the end, she found herself walking away from a brief yet exhilarating moment; a moment in life that would be just a glimpse of the past.

DEMONS

Caught motionless in wet architecture, I moved my numb limbs only to feel possession. Vulnerability turned the demons on me; I, though, deceived them. Beneath the drain lived a dark world and my shower felt as if it washed me towards it. I played the game, and they worshipped me.

My demons brought me closer to manic moments of late nights and racing thoughts. My energy picked up along with my social impulsiveness. I was running through a maze with no map; hoping I would reach the end by following my heart. My free spirit needed restraint but my wild, stubborn character would not be leashed. I lay in bed with my demons only with the desire to forget them and keep going.

They watched from everywhere. She put on a show by grotesquely eating her pasta and leaving her hair uncombed. She couldn't allow them to know the truth and so became one with them. Cigarette butts piled high, and she fell deeper into their misery.

EGGS

The urban farm flourished as she tended to her chickens and collected fresh eggs daily. Used jam jars were filled with honey given by the bees. The young chickens often gave a single egg containing two yolks, symbolic of good luck. The bees sat in a meadow close to the water where there was a dock and boat. The chickens neighbored a gravel driveway. A small farm was brought to a big city, and it thrived.

Her mouth widened and her jaw felt broken as she cracked her way into reality from the dinosaur's shell. She had been a cat before where she could feel purring within her chest and throat. For some reason, that was scarier. Her rib cage opened, and her heartbeat could not be felt when she was an elephant. She felt trapped in an enclosed space and wanted freedom of self again. Her broken mind fought for rebirth.

The scent of cooking onion rose from the crackling skillet as she chopped a tomato and avocado. A mixture of blue and brown eggs sat in a glass cookie jar next to the stove. While she mixed three eggs in a bowl she wondered if she wanted an omelet versus scrambled. She poured the eggs into the skillet and watched them yellow. An omelet it was.

FEET

Coffee shops and boutiques are by my sides, and I'm confused by the friendly gestures as I hold my head high, return them, and become immersed. The cobblestone moves against my newfound Mid-western heels, and I find myself shopping. The high-end thrift store smells of musk and I question the wear of a seemingly new belt. I didn't have to try it on. I place my fingers under a long chain necklace and pull the pendant towards me. It looked cheap and I liked it. The child within me wants one more item and I move towards the shoes. Iowa City's cobblestones were worn and sad from my steps. I laced up and left.

The chapel floors squeaked as I bent over and laced up my All-Star sneakers. I was out of place and felt small with feelings growing. I stepped between the cracks and finally found my way onto one. I was led outside where I pulled out a used plastic water bottle. I played with the cap and twisted the crinkled paper. What I really wanted was limoncello. I scanned the piazza and moved around a motionless stroller towards a café. I sat and placed my feet on the lower table rim. The white stars on my shoes twisted and my feet stretched.

Smoke from the bonfire lifted and I looked upward. The chatter picked up along with the can openers. It was hard to breathe, and my eyes burned. I wanted to be reminded of crying even though it wasn't me. He took my hand and we walked away until we found a new seat on the water's edge. I picked at the sand between my toes and pointed out a subtle wave in the distance. The can in my hand was still warm and I was happy to have a silver spoon. I bounced up and dug my ruined orange toenails into sand that wouldn't be ruined for long.

GREEN

Spring welcomes me with undying support, as my bare legs lay heavy on green grass. The indented marks on the backs of my legs should tell me to move but I am still content. Weeds stick to my hair as I reach towards my melting purse and overheated phone. Summer feels near and the greenery in my pupils reflects my desire for a colorful life.

Her hazel green eyes watched the soccer ball move with speed across turf. The uniforms stood out against the bright field, and she reached towards her own for adjustment. She wore her thick, long hair in a braided ponytail that had been tugged and pulled downwards too many times. Placing a corner kick was exhilarating, especially when the ball penetrated the net. When her green eyes found focus between the field and lit ball, she nailed it.

I stood on top of a mountain in Wyoming. My oversized backpack sat heavy on my chafed hips and my hands rested on the buckle at my waist. The green bandana around my neck protected me from mosquitoes and my socks were worn high on my calves. I reached for my water and sipped sparingly. The view went on indefinitely and I took in the wooded greenery and rolling hills with an appreciation never to be forgotten.

HUNGER

The skin between my jaw line and cheekbones felt thin with hunger and my eye sockets deepened into desire. My face felt raw like a piece of thinly cut prosciutto and I could feel my spine press against the soft couch cushion. The starvation stemmed from an unhealthy mind, but it felt real like the spleen I thought I spread over toast. The torture endured was unbearably painful as I plowed forward and chomped down undesirably disgusting meals.

I brought my plate upstairs to be alone with the warm bagel. It entered my open mouth and saliva dripped from my lips in congruence with mournful tears of missed meals. With each bite came new life but my shrunken stomach and unused jaw called for slow eating. I sobbed my way through chewing with a dreadful moaning face. The sound of desirable pain for food shot through my core and ached deeply within my taste buds. It was heard and I was satisfied.

My hunger for life transcended from experienced charisma that shook my core with laughter and joy. I wanted more. My sporadic energy enveloped others with focus and curiosity. I felt alive and eager to fulfill my hungry character. Life was too good to be wasteful of cherished moments.

ILLUSIONS

My eyes rested on my computer screen and an image of a painting stared back at me. A euphoric burst within my soul brought tears when a vision exploded from the center of the screen and reached my magnetic pupils. Sharp and lucid, the illusion gave meaning to the unfeasible. The movement of vivid colors came to a structured rest, and I would now forever try to make sense of the impossible.

I questioned how the moving shards of light could be a figment of the imagination. They danced above me in resemblance to changing strands of DNA. The opaque energy condensed and then opened into new figures. The room was dark with bursts of light, and I was curious. What were they?

She travelled the planetary system where she found her home in a different place. A cloned vessel of herself resided on Earth along with everyone else. Altered communications between confused minds pushed her further from reality. She became lost in space and time with no one around her. The energy pulled between absences grew into pressured movements amongst those she was surrounded by.

JEWELRY

She walked through the wind and her hair danced around her ears where purple gemstones swayed. Her fur scarf gave comfort to the earrings as they sat upon it with disorientation. She smiled at strangers and clenched her coffee. Her lipstick stuck to the plastic cup, and she caressed her teeth with her tongue. She played with her earrings and smoothed her hair around her ear. Her movement quickened as she held her head high.

Her meticulous hands pinched the wires and pulled them upwards together before quickly wrapping them tightly around the gemstone. She produced handcrafted earrings efficiently and sold her pieces in a few boutiques. Her mother was her biggest supporter, wearing her jewelry daily. She fought to expose her brand but working alone allowed for small enhancements. Maybe she could be at peace with another hobby.

She still wears her gold bumblebee ring. It sits loosely on her right ring finger, held on by a simple gold band. It was handcrafted in a small jewelry store in Rome, Italy. One of the best years of her life was when she called Rome her home and she would go on to get a bumblebee tattoo on her ribcage. Life was too short for a lack of gold bling and the permanence of unforgotten memories.

KNIGHTS

He played the game and pursued the young girl, igniting feelings of a special self within her. Their quiet emails provoked an intimate sense of secret lust. She slept with her phone close to her chest because his messages had found a place in her heart. She thought he had saved her only to learn he would break the person she once was.

My mind tightens around his and I should be more scared. He stays with me through the sharp pains that ping around my brain and make me question reality. The act could get old and fade, but a moment of feelings won't be forgotten. He may move forward with new and used perspectives and I will remain myself. I follow my energy too quickly where I become lost. He has caught me before.

My stubbornness shooed the idea of a knight in shining armor and so he never came. He had tried but I would become lost in an idea of boredom. I was wrong. I was a persistent free spirit who always found myself pursuing first. It had not worked for me yet.

LOVE

Finding myself with giddy and electric pulses moving through my hungry stomach. An acceleration of joy jolts inwardly and I'm excited to wake up from a downward spiral. My face aches from smiling and my eyes pinch to show him I'm there. Visible only in my mind where I run into fear; I sprint forward towards his fireworks.

Her head rests heavy on his bare chest as she moves her hand upward from his ribcage. Serenity is found as her mind clears with a meditative blank gaze towards nothingness. She wonders if his arm has fallen asleep but hesitates to move away from the peaceful moment. Her fingers find his collarbone and pushes herself to awake into a new day of gratitude before reaching towards his scruff.

The dating world exhausted her as desirable candidates dwindled into unions. She passionately strived towards companionship; a happy place of safety where she self-loved. She had been there before but now felt alone with a safety net of single friends. The time would come for another love and her impatience would grow with her aging perspective that was unwinding into chaos.

MEDIA

Lost in a reflection of yourself within others; we strive inward, forward, and then backwards to get an angle of deeply projected performance. A tilt of the chin and a glance in the eye give meaning and persona to an image otherwise still with self-indulgence. Serve your selfie and save your savory looks.

The diagram of my mind's trickery put me at the center. Everyone in my life dispersed from this nucleus and when they did not call upon their own network, the chain of connection stopped at them. Some ignored when they were called to and checked out of the mind space while others grew their networks to where they were communicating with strangers; some of whom were falling in love. I was exposed and vulnerable with my mind effortlessly sharing my life.

I don't read the paper and the little news I watched littered my mind with absurdity. I sat in front of the television but disregarded it as I found focus on my phone. I found my friends' personal news more entertaining than world affairs while knowing the knowledge broadcasted in front of me may be of more importance. Instead, I found productivity in painting. I dismissed the television and phone and walked downstairs where I found escape in a colorful array of acrylics.

NAKED

Exposed to herself, she sat hunched in the shower; water beating down on her head with a wet washcloth laid across her bent knees. Her back pressed against the tile wall, and it felt cooler. She took this time for herself and found refuge in the enclosed steaming space. She placed the warm washcloth over her face and knew this peaceful moment, like any, would not last for long.

Her vulnerability showed sensitivity that was otherwise overlooked but she still smiled with her eyes and kindness got her into trouble. Her stubbornness kept her afloat with a dangerous aspect of self-belief. She would triumph with her vulnerable kind eyes that moved her forward with compassion.

They snatched their clothes from the grass beach and laughed their way through running from the skinny dippers. The dark night caught up with them as they slowed before reaching their parents' house. Seattle summer nights called for teenage mischievousness and hormonally arrogant chatter. They thought they would stay young forever until they were now onlookers of the giddy children.

OPENNESS

My eyes open to find vibrant Seattle light peering through cracked shades. I lie curled on my side yet feel open to the day. My cappuccino waits by the bedside table, and I reach towards it for a sip before melting back into momentary rest. I look out of the window wondering how my drowsy mornings escalade into more productive days.

Her imagination was open to exploration as she stepped from one project to another. The creativity of her mind lacked stability but had adventurous character. Her talents coincided with her impatience for pursuing new endeavors. She was happiest when productive. She remained open, knowing she would find her niche someday.

Opportunity opened only to let go of a past achievement. She pushed herself vigorously forward towards more experience and took pride in her accomplishments. She opened her blank journal where a purple pen found the first page. Not knowing where her open mind would take her next, she simply wrote her name.

PARTIES

She lit up the dance floor with embarrassingly harsh movements but kept confidence and enthusiasm. The night was young and strangers were drawn to her old soul. She felt rhythm pulse through her body as her smile grew and contagiously attracted new dancers. Her fiery movements shook the floor and brought awe and laughter to amused onlookers.

The chatter picked up as they moved along the couch to squeeze in two more people. A coffee table sat sideways with empty beer cans piling across its already scathed and sticky surface. There was no room for cards and so they held the game close to their bodies with a tipsy overflowing spurt of jovial amusement. A small gathering brought big entertainment.

Her long white gown resembled a wedding dress never to be worn on the real day. The tiered feathers brought a funky excitement to the look, and she wore it with pride. She was eighteen years old and her fellow debutante friends would laugh at the irony of their immaturity as they snuck into the kitchen and stole plain bagels. Their first year of college brought weight and dress fittings had been stressful. It was an experience to be remembered.

QUIVERING

My body was pushed to its limits as my next soccer move was perfected in my head. The heat beat down and the hairs on my arms stood up, repelling the warmth from reaching my already overworked body. My lungs worked fiercely as I moved up and down the field. As I recovered, my body shook with shock.

Waves pulse against my pupils and reverse back into his. He feels my euphoric expression's warmth, and I feel his lips tighten only to release. I watch steadily to focus on my face and push to feel what he only knows. He catches me startled given a glimpse into a rare moment. Our mouths open together and separately to be connected passionately at once and in different places. Quivering jaws and tightened eyes meet momentarily until washed away.

She ran from the pool to the hot tub as her body quivered from the cool summer night's breeze. It had been a hot day, but evening temperatures dropped quickly and brought the day's festivities to a closing. Her already few friends began to dwindle, and she sought to be inside. She wrapped the large towel around her damp body and tiptoed with pace up the staircase and towards warmth.

REFLECTING

She saw herself reflected in her sunglasses through the window and looked past the car's outer mirror into cornfields. The drive gave her time to reflect on what was left behind and the new adventure to come. After a nap it was her turn to drive. She cruised steadily through the flat grounds and would look forward to reaching the clear heated blurs that waited in the distance. Her nerves spiked with the thought of the heavy trailer carried behind. Cars passed and her life was moving forward into unknown territory. The heat burned off and the sun faded. She removed her sunglasses and glanced in the mirror. She rolled down the window and looked out onto the cornfields.

She lived in her own world and almost missed the bus. She found a spot and hesitated to touch the greasy metal bar that no longer had a clear reflection. There would be two stops that disrupted her morning thought process. People clung to themselves as more pushed and shoved to enter. The windows were scratched, and the bus jolted through the winding streets. The first bus ride came to an end with many more to come.

Her nose touched the sun and her eyes laughed under her hat. It was summer but it always felt that way. She laid back, pushed her legs forward and tilted the rim of her sun hat over her already shaded eyes. She gazed down but the reflections of the water against her sunglasses lit up. She was thoughtless, in the moment, yet knew a life reflection was brewing. Pulling herself to her feet and tossing her sunglasses aside, she walked towards the water where her eyes met him.

STORES

Finding my way from comfort to cabinet and caught in a flurry of open bright space. Pillowcases encompass my bright eyes and I move upward towards more. A glimpse in a mirror and I catch the soft blankets in my reflection. I want to rest forever on a coach I cannot afford. Give me texture; I feel it all.

I was a candy girl. I wore a pink apron and greeted customers with sweet eyes. The store smelled of sugar and colorful candies filled glass jars with elegant lids. I tasted the new gummies when the store was empty and gave mixtures of them to children who selected excitedly with pointed fingers. They brought cash and the register was filled with change. My candy girl career was short lived, but I would frequently go back for candy of my own.

Shopping was never my favorite activity, but the outcome brought me new looks that made me get up in the morning.

I reached towards the tags to read the red inked numbers only to quickly move onto the next item. The oversized orange sweater stood out and I pulled it over my shirt. I always only needed to try one piece on before checking out.

TWINS

Reflected in the mirror she saw him looking back at her; their faces becoming one. Confused but not frightened, she questioned the connection to this past love who now encompassed the visual perception of herself. She fought to discover, and her mind created a narrative to put the chaos of her wonderings at ease. For her, they were connected from the beginning.

Two within one and connected by conception, they sat heavy in the skillet. The egg had been larger and so she knew the possibility of a double yolk within. The yolks barely touched and took up more space as they spread throughout the pan. She would only need one egg for her meal.

The twin stroller carried the infants down the leaf dirtied path. Their matching hats and shoes kept them warm during the brisk fall walk. I only caught a glimpse as their mother pushed them by me strongly. I would look though and wonder if my life would bring such gifts.

UNIFORMS

The cart came bolting towards her, as she stood frozen on the tarmac. She was friendly and aloof to the men in uniform who arrived at the scene. They rummaged through her luggage and asked questions while she stayed psychotically in her missioner mind. That night was spent in Los Angeles where she did not sleep or eat. She would be found the next day before being released and roaming the streets with her frenzied and lonely mind.

They hung their sweaty uniforms and sprayed them with scented disinfectant. The humidity stained their white jerseys yellow, and soccer was played daily in them. The sports academy logo sat boldly on both the shorts and shirt of the uniform, and I felt pride.

She mingled drunkenly with the fleet of cops outside the beer festival. She found humanity beneath their strict uniforms, and they liked her. She told them of times when she had not been on good terms with their kind, and they laughed. Beneath the badges were heartfelt perspectives.

VOICES

Buzzing bees swarmed her mind before the clarity of a single man's voice persisted to ask, "Are you there?" They knew each other and she felt safe in the privacy of her most shamed moments. From morning to night, they spoke of such nonsense from lunch to toilet paper. Trust grew and she loved him only to be heartbroken when saying goodbye and returning to health.

She was in choir as a child and now regularly found herself at a high-end karaoke bar. Her voice was no longer angelic and tuned from training, but music still brought her overwhelming feelings of bliss. The bar gave privacy to their singers with individual rooms set up for small groups. Frequenting weekly, they knew the songs they were going to sing. Choir left a mark on her, but her voice would take her nowhere but the high-end karaoke bar.

The voices in her mind were not muffled nor distorted. The pitch and tones were exactly of those sounds she heard from those she knew, and she questioned how it could not be them. They spoke to her, and she responded with indifference. She might be psychotic, but she knew the sounds swarming her mind were those of figments of the imagination.

WATER

The dealership felt open after the windows were cleaned. Soap separated and was washed away only to be brought out by the harsh weather. I looked through the glass and saw a bored woman kick a puddle. The attendant rubbed his hands with a damp washcloth before entering the vehicle. Tires turned and a used car was sprayed and dirtied with mud soon to be washed away. The car wash cycled quickly. I peeked into the back where water was drained into the center of a cement ground. Everything was left behind, including my used car.

———

I moved backwards as my head lifted. A line formed and my thirst quickened. The fountain looked elegant and gave me water. I nudged the bottle into my oversized bag where it found a home between olive oil and stationery. The remnants of vitamin C powder shook and dissolved as I stepped quickly across the bridge and to the bus stop. I heard the shaking within my bag and the water beneath me.

———

My mind drifted and my ears opened to the fair distance. My mouth watered as I thought of cotton candy and kettle corn. Sunscreen was reapplied and slipped off my body as I went to and from the water. My book curled from damp fingertips and my eye squinted as I shook the inside of my ear. My sweat pearled and sat for too long. I'd rather be sitting with water.

X-RATED

Impregnated with scurrying cockroaches that moved against her innards; still and then crawling up her throat after triggering bites of needed food. The pig fetus sat low and moved more slowly. Her head ached and body repelled the creatures not meant to be growing within a body that now seemed a mere science project. She felt it as her reality with her stomach growing and moving, transitioning into new species.

Blood ran down her legs and she couldn't find peace in the spirits. They brutalized her and she felt lost in a hopeless place. She lay curled on her side with nothing to protect herself from the invisible pressure. She felt as if she left her wounded marks wherever she traveled. She sat on the white couch and said nothing.

She stood frozen in the shower with what she thought was blood running off her. She turned only to feel her sliced back burn from the warm water. Her tortured mind had reached her body and what she knew as her reality seemed impossible. She dried herself with a towel only to be covered with blood once again.

YARDS

I was never one to garden but my three plant pots flourished on the deck that overlooked the well-seeded lawn. The fireflies and sparks from the fire lit up the yard with a home feeling. I reminisced on my soccer days by buying a ball and kicking it around. Your first yard is a good one.

As I slid along the highway in a paralyzed state of shock, my face lit up with sparks and my body cringed into a protective cocoon. Grasping the car's inner handle, I pushed my body away from the gravel that shot up from the ground. For the 200 yards that I slid along the road, I knew one thing: I was going to live. The smell of tar emulated the enclosed space as we hurriedly pulled ourselves free through the trunk. Exhaustion came over my body as I stared at the empty window frame and twisted seat I had occupied.

She took her journal to a tree enclosed space where she laid down a blanket and got lost in her mind. The yard sat next to a golf course and as the sun went down, we moved onto it and ran through the sprinklers. We awoke the neighbors from our nighttime hot tubs when we would dare to run around the snow-covered house. Summer and winter, this is a place of joy and escape.

ZOMBIES

They roamed the streets with short, harsh movements and deathly faces. She limped as she pushed the shopping cart up the street, but it didn't seem she was in pain. Their heads tilted and behind their eyes was absence. I kept to myself as I feared for my life.

My starved brain sucks life from my body as I plow forward with intent. My jaw tightens and drool pools in my mouth only to overflow with agony; the liquid spills and my pressured temples cannot capture the dribble. The decayed feeling in my mouth overwhelmed my usually smooth teeth that now felt spaced and jagged. Being close to death meant a grotesque ache for life.

I did not care for television or reading and stared robotically at my computer screen. Fire and tea sat in front of me and gave me warmth. The wild puppy had found a moment of peace and sat to my right with the occasional scurry across my keyboard. My glasses gave my usual contact irritated eyes a rest and inspiration were brewing. Coming through my deadened motivation and into life, I found my stiff hands typing once again. I wonder what they will write.

POETRY:

Part IV

In the shadows of the Devine
You rock me
My stomach
Where all is fine
Envelop my body
Take over my confusion
Reach my heart
That pumps the lullaby

The one that rocks
And rocks
The path

The path that leads
To the song
That succeeds

The song that
Sings to my stomach

The song that
Keeps you close

The song that
Makes us whole

Come rock with me

My rock

My love

My forever

Lullaby

We feel our bodies as we feel our brains. We are seen by our mind's perceptions – a reflection of ourselves in others – an idea of our worthiness in self.

We sell our bodies as objects – we bathe in materials – we mold expression and language into a physical metaphor of feeling. We ask ourselves… What do I look like?

We hide – we pretend – we become consumed. Why?

Our bodies serve the universe – not the beauty within our souls. Our bodies work for others and not the passion that fuels our inspiration.

Let shame devour itself.

We are beautiful.

Eagles – they dive – what a burden.

They soar – crowns held high.

They know the sharks are there.

They watch – until the owl arrives.

They fetch a glance.

At the ducks.

They know who they are.

Their howl reaches the puppy.

Their bark laughs at stupidity.

The owl feels stupid.

So – who am I?

Sweep me up.

Carry me with you.

Snatch my heart.

Fill my lungs.

Move my body.

Let me share with you.

Take note of the electricity. It binds the poem of sound. It stabs with the knife.

The cross tuned. Rotate me.

Where is my heart?

You will become the shape of your choice – the color that blends effortlessly into a textured life.

You will become patterned with inspiration – your engine will effortlessly move you forward into a deep and untouchable awareness.

I will roll out the carpet.

Just walk the line.

My peace
a piece
of paper
that blew away
and in its dance
God grabbed hold

and round
and round
spun me

into his open heart
where his arms felt hands
where his knees felt the floor

he then reads from the paper

indescribable words
that filtered into my mind
as a language
meant for us

I will forever try to understand

but why?

the vibration

the electricity in my dance
the light

I feel all of you

Grab my hands
twirl me
swirl me into your soul

my soul
ours

See me with your magic

shine

I am losing myself. I am finding the secret and gusty gardens in the mind of collection.

A lonely place where longing to see eyes sparkle and grin – to see smiles unwind into pure expression – appears as a fleeting memory.

I am homesick.

I surrender. Not to life but to power – and to grief. I see sadness and I see hope.

Don't both mean the same for me?

There is only one weapon I have not found – it sits in disbelief. It is piercing. Break me.

Its sparklers radiate my mind. The changing paths lead me to an empty idea.

Let me close the door.

Let me reach it.

Let me touch it.

Wear it.

Its symbol gives me strength with a shine that disperses – light my trail.

Recognize me.

Maybe it's safer being alone in this place.

Maybe the doctor scares me.

Maybe the beach bores me.

Love soars with me to unknown territories, and I surrender to fear.

I trust the ink that bleeds.

The ballpoint pen spins to the grasp my hand feels.

I cry – what do I feel?

I see deformity in my body.

I see play.

I see a stampede of the impossible.

At this very moment I grasp the present vision.

A vision of you.

In the comforts of my mind.

The dinosaurs didn't scare me. I heard their passion. I trusted them.

The cat was flawless. Its pink dress was timeless.

The poster was untouchable. I kissed it every night.

My mind was born – an invitation was sent.

My room opened as my youthful heart pranced towards the entrance.

I unlocked my bedroom – my safe space.

It crawled in and drew a fort.

I thought I was safe.

Safe to create.